The Paris Hours

Collected Poems

HEATHER NEFF

The Paris Hours
Collected Poems

Copyright © Heather Neff (2022)

ISBN 9798841263708

Cover photograph by Heather Neff

Interior portrait of Heather Neff by Jacques Lampécinado

Author's Note

Acelebrated novelist once said in an interview that he found dialogue easy to write because he didn't create his characters, he *became* them.

I have found this to be more true than I've been comfortable admitting to others. It is often as difficult to finish a novel as it is to leave someone you deeply love. This has, however, not been my experience with poetry—which is strange, because it is through loving poetry that I first fully understood my need to dedicate my life to literature. Yes, I've read books avidly from the time I was a child, marveling at the sanctuary from daily life they offered me. But no, I don't remember feeling that I would make writing my vocation until, fifty years ago, my close friend Alice Peck shared with me "The Love Song of J. Alfred Prufrock."

We were fifteen years old. It was summer; we were in her room, and she produced a tattered grey paperback edition of T.S. Eliot's *The Waste Land and Other Poems* (I still have the book), and we read it, forehead to forehead, in muted voices, as if it were a clandestine, forbidden thing. The lines became a secret language we shared, and even though I had never left the United States, I had a deep visual impression of London, of Prufrock, and of those mermaids riding the waves in a roiling grey sea.

And I wanted to write poetry.

Time has shown me that I was born to the squalor of the novel and not to the economy of verse, but I nonetheless gather here some of the words I've corralled into something like poetry, because I fear that if I'm not careful, they'll take their freedom and might never again be found.

The poems in this collection represent a distinct phase of my life. *The Paris Hours*, written during my sojourn in France (1979-1981), includes both free verse and a number of poems set to music and kept deliberately simple in their rhyming structure for ease of performance.

I see these poems now as prayers to the morning, noon, and evening of my life, celebrations of moments too fleeting, like smoke, to grasp with one's mind. They are part of the ritual of remembrance—the hope that something of the past will always remain.

Heather Neff, 2022

Poems

Sarah	1
Algerian Wife at Beaubourg	4
L'Invalide	5
Chloe's Song	6
last tango	7
Habib	10
Esquisses du Luxembourg	11
Bassam	13
Acis and Galatea and the Birds	14
Song for David	15
Aileen	17
Sevres Babylon	18
Rembrandt	19
The Wedding	20
you know	22
Fortune	23
Aubade	25

Cortege   28

it wasn't you   29

the rush for love   30

Café Maghreb   31

Childhood   34

Choice   35

Vincennes   36

These Days   37

Paname   38

Sarah

You must meet my woman
he said
and I pondered who would live with
his stained fingers
yellow teeth
unwashed hair and
morte subite

Then I climbed eight flights
to the *chambres de bonnes*
under the rue des archives'
stained copper roofs

and found

your eyes

Modigliani face
eclipsed from simple grace
and a voice to calm a child

calmed the child in me
who'd begun to wonder
why I was even alive

Your certainties:

poverty was a necessity
you would learn Russian
and he would write

bought his cigarettes and beer
and his talk about himself
in the American bar at midnight

For you believed in him
trusted his pen
and the rice you ate
the cats that shared
the fleas of your love-damp bed.

Convened, I taught you English and
you taught me French and
sometimes you came and
showered at my place

Took me for tea and cake and
did what you could to thank me
for not judging

But how could I judge,
when you were giving me

My   Self

While we spoke softly
on rain-warmed afternoons
beneath the copper roof

a love song

composed of   our dreams.

Sarah   my first teacher,
you taught me to teach
taught me the awe
of teaching others

and found me lovely
beyond my rage
self-hate
my groveling sense of

Obligation.

We lost each other
when you went home
to celebrate your Bac

and I left my borrowed room
for yet another
when I came back to find you
you had moved on   too

Thirty years later I found him
writing
now author   noted critic   professor

But when I discovered you

Sarah

a name in a phone book
I didn't have the courage to call you.

I have done so much more
than I ever dreamed
on those gray afternoons
on the rue des archives

and yet   and yet

I have not yet become

even a shadow
of the woman
you believed I was

November 18, 2007 - December 30, 2021

Algerian Wife at Beaubourg

She stands near the crowd
fingers deep in babies' hands,
hennaed hair sun white

1979

L'Invalide

Someone whistling nine floors below
Feels cold water seethe from a hose and
break upon his hands on its plunge
to the flowers.

He cannot know the task of these lungs
to suck in air and release it.

The whistling becomes the lines of a song,
the geraniums are crisp and strong
beside this man's mangled words
and the fierceness of his eyes
that watch mine
to see if he has become
a plant or a song

or a monster.

Nine floors below the planting goes on
and the water flows and the song
has its motion —
yet what motion

Beside this man undefined
who lies poised
on the weight of

a gasp?

1980

Chloe's Song

She walks silently with her hands buried,
Wading through waves of red and gold leaves,
The dream-crossed twilight beckoning, beckoning,
She tastes a trace of summer on the breeze.

Somehow she recalls in the glowing fall
A sweet sense of intangible things,
When one passes over, calling, calling
The frontier of the spirit's safety —

To find herself alone
Beyond all limits of day
When sound and sight and question
Become an echoing phrase

Instinctively she hears the lovers' sighs
Feels the blind man's cane tapping her soul
Through the coming night, falling, falling
So close that it kisses her brow.

Strange realities, possibilities,
Hung like spiders' webs, drifting like smoke,
Through the autumn fires, swirling, swirling
She senses it
She feels it
She knows.

1980

last tango

detroit
saturday night
and he didn't call
so
i set out
in tight jeans (even tighter sweater)
to cobb's tavern

to find him

and there he was
with another woman (broad and plain)
a friend he said
i could come with them

to see the film
they'd already chosen

and i

jealous & defiant
went to see
exactly what he
saw in her

but instead discovered

paris
apartment above the river
rue jules verne
beside the bridge

trains passing,
sensual abandon

dance of heat and death
in the afternoon

jeanne
fur-collar   flowered hat
tall boots   dark thatch

jeanne
in white satin
and wet curls
full paps

and, with jeanne, i
learned of

altars (of flesh)
betrayals (of lovers)
biers (of beloveds)

And in two short hours that left me

gutted

i became jeanne and
she
unchained me:

yes, there have been others
whom i loved without loving

but never again
have i been quite so
willing

to give myself
blindly

or wait
without knowing

November 17, 2007

Habib

Sand tones frame the dreams of your black eyes,
Sands blown north to hypnotize,
And the sunbaked houses cleared away
So the past becomes a mirage

What is the marrow of survival —
The metal palms and neon sun?
Slavery, supplication,
The sweetness, sweetness of the lie.

There is no fear left in a people without hope,
No moment of surrender,
No waking at the dawn,

Only the prism of raw black force,
This color without shade,
Sand currents
giving depth and tone.

1980

Esquisses du Luxembourg

flute of thick-chopped *frites*
moutarde amputation sharp
tongue brain tear-filled eyes

rough coil lifts in flight
beats the air to swirling cream
periwinkle wings

Jean-Michel and Paul
pale Mireille and Chantal
childhood's anxious thrall

shredding white-barked trunks
host a velvet anarchy
dappled sunlit moss

sailboats basin bound
launched by bamboo-guided hands
grandpere's hourglass dreams

tattered Sistine skies
cobalt silk on ashen clouds
ride the dying storm

blankets of eiffels
Europe's covert supplicants
flee at gendarmes' sight

metal chairs have eyes
measuring the chance to seize
quick hot take-out love

basil lavender
melon fig jasmine ices
heaven at the gates

noiseless hour of night
fountain whispers over stone
secrets to the dawn

Hemingway wrote here
Pound and Eliot and Stein
but it's Heather's now

1979–2022

Bassam

Froasted glasses breed dreams of Lebanon,
Swimming in an azure sea of
lemon whiskey poetry and
pinball rhythms.

You know your knee presses mine
and the other knee keeps time
to music squeezed from
numbered machines:

Weaving up your city
fringed by ornate palms
You promise arabesques if I'll come.

You know
This all leads to nothing
Except perhaps the hope that drink
Becomes the sap of Romance
Instead of lonely coupling.

And our cafe is quiet but for

rambling voices and ice cubes
whispering to frosted glasses
in exasperation.

November 15, 1979

Acis and Galatea
and the Birds

The pigeons dip their heads and
        iridescent wings,
settled, contented with
mechanical purrs
inside the autumn leaves

Bowing politely before marble lovers
whose eyes never leave one another,
Poised on a graceful marble breast
or marble curls that coolly rest

A nervous sparrow joins the basin,
then several more who flutter furious:
The pigeons soothingly ignore them,
The morning sun shines in.

A great bronze god looms startled and angry
to see the silent, sensuous couple,
Yet still doesn't mind the pigeon
perched on his head, watching for trouble —

And the beat of flaming silver wings
laced with black and blue and
white will brush
the lips and slender hips
in sudden rush.

1979

Song for David

I can still see the lights from the tourist boat
turning the water to gray,
standing above the wall on the river
and watching night cover the day.

Oh, David, remember, we had no reflection,
the current just passes us by,
and life, like the gold tip of each rolling wave
mirrors the light in our eyes.

When will we ever be wise?

I still believe you wanted to kiss me,
but all our fear kept us apart,
Soft goodbyes strewn on a wind-beaten Sunday,
November surrounding our hearts —

Oh, David, remember, we had no reflection,
Only the dreams we ignore,
And Life, who will not give us anything more
waits in a patient disguise,

When will we ever be wise?

David, my friend, if you will consider
Then all of these things will come clear:
I still believe the love lives inside us
Remember the joy, not the fear!

Oh, David, remember, we had no reflection,
The moments grow sharper with time,
And Life, like the gold waves that flowed on beneath us,
lives on in these sad, searching rhymes.

When will we ever be wise?

1979, 2006

Aileen

like a vein of violet
in the cusp of an orchid
her beauty blooms

in her smile the echo
of a seashell's song, of
sunlight in a silent room

in her eyes the amber smoke
of her ancestors' dawns,
wisdom of the mountains
ranging far and long

she moves on a seagull's wing
the gentle Aileen
far, far away from her home

1981

Sevres Babylon

Silver-haired monsieur in London Fog
steps off the metro
umbrella handle loops his collar
the spokes a compass
to his heart.

Ignoring the staring crowds
pouring around him
he smiles,
eyes bright with

plaisirs volés

1980

Rembrandt

Cleft between brows
furrowing
source of light
fading curls
trembling, knotted hands

Before an easel,
hair scarved away
from hollow eyes —

painted for no one to see,
the portrait
remembers

Confidence

June 9, 1980

The Wedding

Sitting across from his thick fingers
watching the crackling flames in his eyes
I wonder how much closer to paradise
I will ever come,
how much longer, like Hagar, I would seek
a true and lasting home.

We come to the house in the fog
mount stairs to rooms heady with propane,
walls of faded flowers
and a kitchen of flowing laughter.

In the cellar a ring of men slaughter a
skittering sheep,
the blood draining as they speak in taut voices,
while in the flat above the sisters
pack boxes with sugar-dusted treats,
curls pressed together
whispers of the nuptial night

His mother wears earrings of ceramic
lapis-gold hints of a different world,
when their people formed families of mountain stone.
Her hawk-cries pierce the night-cold air
with longing for the sea and sky and home.

His father's robe molds his hips
when tightly bound with a knotted scarf,
one shoulder rises, the other answers
the music takes his body
hair flickering silver in the low lamplight

He guides me from the room of rough-skinned men
into the fields outside the celebration

He wraps a scarf over my hair:
Tu est belle, he says
perhaps dreaming me into their mountains
sun-seared skies, gold-green waters
In this late-winter twilight the grass is blue
the air laden with love

Doe-eyed and white-laced, the bride and groom kiss,
the groom she'd seen once before
beneath the gaze of three sisters
her mother father
and her brother

My lover.

We toss rice and rose petals
then sit with thighs touching,
eating rich steaming mutton
sesame cakes
couscous with butter

I came to your home afraid
of the blood-depth in your mother's song,
afraid of the void your sisters would see in my eyes —

I who have no songs to sing, no dances to share
the tattered stars and stripes and my
rootless soul

And left this cusp of unriddled kindness
with a strange sense of being
Whole

March, 1980

you know

You know it's never long enough to open up your heart,
but it's never short enough to close your eyes to pain,
and there's always perfect timing to tear down your wall of caution
and to press the tide of feeling till you break —

and you know its never long enough to answer all your questions,
but you always find a reason to set aside your pride
and although it's always over when it hardly has begun,
you didn't have to fool yourself, you didn't have to lie —

but you do, you always do —
until the moment when his footsteps
disappear down the hall
and the echo of his touch
is all

is all.

Well, you know it's never real enough to cast away your past,
but it's never false enough to make this dream your last
and you always find the time enough
to justify the reasons why you never really love.

1980

Fortune

The gypsy woman
of the June solstice days
finds me in the foyer
41 rue des Archives,
her warm wine breath
traces arcs across my palm

She enters in a sunlit shaft from
the rain-greyed afternoon,
grasps my hand with the
strength of a will
that snuffs
the cloistered air between us

I see the flowered dress,
hear the rough-smoked voice
filled with future memories
of secret pasts.

The gape-teeth smile
I cannot meet her eyes
she knows it
and is well satisfied.

Calm and urgent and mightier than
I will ever be
she breathes in my fear
her dry finger reads me

A long life, ninety-six years!
Your worries of your family are not grave
And your recent operation
is all finished
But you will have an invitation of marriage,
A proposal
A problem of two men
one brown, like you, the other, clear —
A voyage in the near future,
And then a deep contentment

But be careful of the women far away
There are women
who are jealous
far away

She waits, her smile vanished with the sun
and her hard grasp tightens until
she feels the coin
fumbled from my
hand-mended jeans

A cinq franc piece
hard earned
quickly given:
Not *cassoulet*, perhaps,
but at least *vin rouge*

and a pittance to pay
for my

Future

June, 1980

Aubade

I leave my love at dawn   take a train to the Madeleine,
this misnamed church   this hulking wreck,
pillared pile of shadows
       No grace for the sacred
       sinner.

And walk until St. Augustine looms ahead,
temple of a deity too tired to care
just across the square from
       the monument to Mars,
        our true God

Haussman's boulevard leads to the sepulcher
of Louis and his child-bride, Austrian Marie,
bronze-roofed and guarded by thick young trees
       making a mock
       of their stolen splendor.

Two cats   black and orange blurs
streak out from the bushes
on some shared mission
       and freeze to statues beneath
       my Medusa stare.

Across the street the stone relief
shark, elephant, tiger crushing a serpent,
       parrots and a crocodile, I think
       voici the vestiges of hard-lost colonies.

At the office near the Opera, I gather up my mail
and descend the Avenue to the Tuileries.
Three red fire trucks, sirens hushing the traffic
            converge on the stone house
               behind me.

Beneath the arch in the wings of the Louvre
I read of Detroit, New York, Ann Arbor,
worlds too far and far too vague
            to find focus on that day

Yet down the steep stairs to the deep stone quais
lined with dark houseboats and rusting barges
and a canopy of white frothing branches

a ghost of Hiroshige
            speaks to me

At the Place Dauphine I shun the Cité with those
shadowed arches and soul-searing windows
and choose St. Germain as a sure pathway
            to the measured peace
               of the Luxembourg, where

Gray-white sunshine pierces spiked walls of trees
olive men in overalls toss handfuls of seeds
on naked beds eroded by winter
            while others gild
               the ancient carousal.

A pair inside the cafe lace fingers
a blond man in black reads Le Figaro,
the smoke from his Gitane stroking
            the swirling plume
               of his cafe-au-lait

I greet the gendarme by the gate
and he smiles and answers, unconcerned
by the water
        that weeps in the basin
        a few feet away

On the Boulevard St. Michel I pause to read
the marble plaques to the citizens fallen
for the liberation of Paris
        And I think
        of only one Citizen

At last, crossing the street
to enter the rue Henri Barbusse
I come to number forty-two
        and pause   because
        this day,

        On this day

        Jean Paul Sartre
        is dead.

April 15, 1980

Cortege

They passed in thousands
The streets stopped, but no horn
blew

All in silence
The car piled high with blossoms
and the air thick with
footsteps and sighs.

They passed through the
grey noon
into their
memories
of him.

Thousands,
heads held high.

In honor of Jean-Paul Sartre, April 23, 1980

it wasn't you

at first, it was your friend
whose quiet grace halted my pace —

most nights I climbed the rue St. Jacques
to avoid *les dragueurs* of St. Michel

but you caught my eye and bowed,
said *bon soir, mademoiselle,*

and your dancing green eyes
eclipsed his sun.

were you teaching him how
in France it is done

how honeyed skin attracts the
sleek Parisian, only to find

yourself faced by a wary,
amused American?

it matters little now,
forty years gone

I don't wonder that you
became my husband

I only ask when,
if ever, my love for you

will ever end?

2021

the rush for love

the rush for love sprouts in the pregnant
pause
between autumn fade and
first snowfall,
when all seek goodwill, the
peace and joy of
a willing companion
on a holy night.

Inside the gardens of the brain
hope roots, watered with a desire
too fierce to ignore
and how we search the evening streets
those Gauloise-end retreats
adrift with tattered lives
and scraps of souls

and how it quells in the
union of skins
elastic and whole
until lips brush eyelids,
with whispered departures,
leaving the stain,
subservient, sour
a memory of the loneliness
that was its birth
before its annunciation.

October 15, 1979

Café Maghreb

drumbeats on a night that is not quite summer
the singer scales Atlas summits from
the depths of his throat
gliding like falcon wings
across a Berber sunset
cooling hot sands to shadow

drums throb on a hidden street, a dark room
flanked by feline-filled windows and antennaed voices,
city noises in a midnight rhythm;
the dark street opens and closes
to the Atlas wanderers

drumbeats rend and soothe
sirens horns rattling Metro
blue trucks filled with homeless men and women
wine-steeped bitter throng

drumbeats drip night from the plaster,
the close sweat of men,
splattering handclaps wells of flesh
blooming at the pits and cleft of thighs,
salt rhythms keeping time

a dog on the tiles, twitching brows wary eyes,
touches his tongue to the floor and
beats his tail, flanks damp and dripping maw

drumbeat meets the smoke stink and yellow mist
words half-formed and lingering
on the pulse of the skin
the music sucked expelled by the breath
of weary womanless men

and she circles arms raised hands
weaving memories of home
shirts open   hard chests glisten
naked wet eyes squinted hypnotism
one calls out another snaps his fingers
hips pound the dark sandals stomp the damp
some lock hands above heaving shoulders
others stare seeing nothing

the woman swathed explosion of scarlet
licks the face of a man and spins away
scarves clinging to thrusting hips
face small and brown with khol-lashed baiting

another with arched full tongue
teasing pouting promise of her smile
black hair painted to her cheeks
she rolls her breasts lifts her hands

a wine glass lies broken near
a table rocking legs weak
elbows pounding and swaying knees
bearded men shout
the woman's hips flick
singer trills
drummer rolls
feet pound
mated round

some feel the breeze and the sea
some know the mystery of coupling
some mourn those far away
and deep holy days when
the body is given
to release
after pain

dusk midnight dawn
drown

in this pitching plunge
of sound

June 11, 1980

Childhood

A child is sacred.
Touch her gently.
Hold her in wonder and
See though her eyes.
Guide her with love,
Teach her with wisdom,
Honor her courage,
Make her your pride.

December 1979

Choice

She has taken the way of the Self,
the head over heart,
the heart that loves.

Whatever I do will hurt you.
If I come to you, I will not stay.
If I do not come
then you will know at last
that it's over.

And it is over.

Except in my heart,
which bleeds each night for you
I hear your voice, touch your hair,
taste your mouth, smell your skin
your golden skin.

And the blotted sound of a name
between smothered sobs
jerks me back from a fitful sleep
and wounds again
the heart that still loves.

I cannot choose another way.
The decision was made long ago,
even before the realization

And until my love begins to fade
I cannot, dare not, will not
see you again.

January 23, 1984

Vincennes

The sun grows cold,
the frost returns,
I hear the birds sing soft to the winter
As leaves turn to gold;
And in the night a glowing moon
Pipes Virgo's tune,
Our lives rush before
the rising tide.

You've touched my heart
I see the youth within your eyes
And know its strong longing
To search free and far,
The time for love
Runs swift and sweet
On Summer's feet
Come, dance while the echo
Still rings clear!

September, 1979

These Days

I am going to tell you the secret of secrets. Death comes and goes about her work through mirrors... Look in a mirror all your life and you'll see Death at work like bees in a glass hive.

— Jean Cocteau

These days are finished forever,
the Paris hours, the dream time
when every emotion came in rhyme
and seconds poured like honey

Gone for now and forever
a sculpted face hardened with age
lost in mirrors smoked with the rage
of a womanchild seeking her way

And now a new path must be found
to equal, perhaps, other hopes and dreams
and so, with courage and hope and trust
She emerges, strong and sound.

September 6, 1984

Paname

She lies there waiting
can you understand
the overwhelming nudity
So sure and unplanned—

With that eternal rhythm so sensual and free,
impossible to count it
existing subtly—
Paris will not articulate
her fine calligraphy,
And you are left to translate
her elusive reality...

Of jumbled rooftops and strangers' eyes
accordion tones and gray wool skies
stairwells' resonance and statue smiles
A gargoyle's sneer o'er miles and miles

Rainclouds holding down the Seine
dried leaves drift like lonely men
Montmartre in the silent night
all of Paris under her sight

Roasted chestnut, *vin rouge* memories
Pigalle's women tell their stories
The Tour Eiffel a point in the night
the steps of Passy endlessly high!

The Louvre with the jewels of centuries
Her garden of dreams, the Tuileries,
Notre Dame timelessly lifting her towers,
The Conciergerie counting the hours.

Clichy and Belleville, the Palais Chaillot,
Chatelet, Montparnasse of long ago,
Menilmontant, Denfert Rochereau,
the muted sound of a tango...

Oh, she laughs and cries and sleeps –
Sometimes sighs and sometimes weeps,

And waits, Eternal.

1979–1980

B orn in Akron, Ohio, Heather Neff's family moved to Detroit when she was in her teens. After graduating from Cass Technical High School, Neff earned a bachelor's degree in English with High Distinction at the University of Michigan. She went on to study French language and culture at the Sorbonne, University of Paris. Neff earned her Lizentiat and doctoral degree in English Language and Literature, Comparative Literature and French Linguistics at the University of Zurich in Switzerland. Neff subsequently spent two years in St. Croix, U.S. Virgin Islands, where she taught at the University of the Virgin Islands and St. Joseph High School. Neff joined the faculty in the Department of English at Eastern Michigan University in 1993, retiring as an Emerita Professor in 2021.

To learn more about Heather Neff's life and work, visit her official author's website: **www.heathernefbooks.net** , or email her at heatherneffauthor@gmail.com .

Novels

Blackgammon

Wisdom

Accident of Birth

Haarlem

Leila: The Weighted Silence of Memory

Leila II: The Moods of the Sea

Blissfield

Saffron Bloom

Audiobook

Accident of Birth (Recorded Books)

Non-fiction

Redemption Songs: Protest in the Poetry of Afro Americans

Poetry

The Paris Hours: Collected Poems

Vespers

Poetry and Short Stories

Unsquared (collection by 826Michigan)

Whittaker Road Works: Departures (editor)

Whittaker Road Works II: Taking Flight (editor)

Whittaker Road Works III: Soaring (editor)

Whittaker Road Works IV: Horizons (editor)